52 WEEKS AMONG THE BEST SELLERS

Yes sir! For 52 weeks this book was stored in a warehouse AMONG THE BEST SELLERS. But now that the best sellers are gone it's time for this book to come out too. So PLEASE . . . BUY IT! We'd hate to have it sent back to that dingy old warehouse for another year among some best sellers.

Al Jaffee
MEETS
HIS END

by

Al Jaffee

A SIGNET BOOK
NEW AMERICAN LIBRARY
TIMES MIRROR

SIGNET TRADEMARK REG. U.S. PAT. OFF. AND FOREIGN COUNTRIES
REGISTERED TRADEMARK—MARCA REGISTRADA
HECHO EN CHICAGO, U.S.A.

SIGNET, SIGNET CLASSICS, MENTOR, PLUME and
MERIDIAN BOOKS
are published by The New American Library, Inc.,
1301 Avenue of the Americas, New York, New York 10019

First Printing, September, 1979

1 2 3 4 5 6 7 8 9

PRINTED IN THE UNITED STATES OF AMERICA

INTRODUCTION

You probably wonder, as most people do, how a wonderful book like this comes into existence. The answer is quite simple. A wonderful book like this comes into existence through tireless effort, unstinting dedication, and unmitigated gall.

In addition, enormous amounts of genius, talent, and physical beauty are required on the author's part. Not to mention modesty and humility.

But enough of this self-effacement. Let's get to your problem, which is how you can produce a wonderful book like this too. Never mind you're no genius and have no talent. Never mind you have no physical beauty or humility. What you do have is our help. All you need to start with is pencil, paper, and a willingness to risk total humiliation.

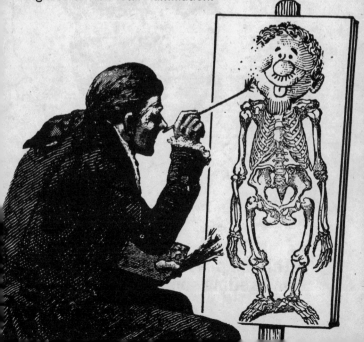

Lesson #1

How to get ideas for a wonderful book like this.

The most important thing about getting funny ideas is to think funny. Here are two examples of funny thinking.

This chap is thinking funny and getting some funny ideas.

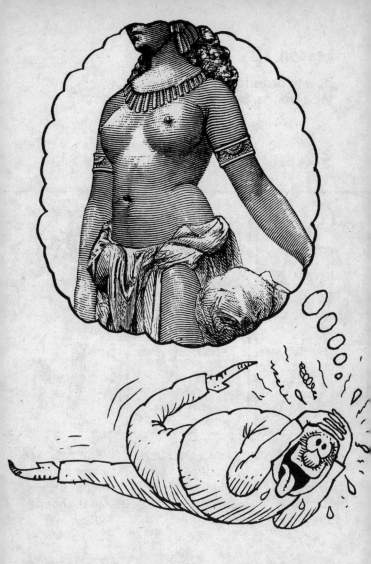

**This chap is not thinking funny but
he's getting some funny ideas anyway.**

Lesson #2

How to draw funny pictures for a wonderful book like this.

A lot of people think drawing funny is difficult. Well it isn't if you know how. By following the simple steps shown below you can easily master this problem.

Start with a simple funny stick figure of the human body . . .

Add a few funny features to fill out the human body . . .

And *voilá!* You have a truly funny drawing of the human body.

Well, now we've shown you how to think funny and draw funny. But we still don't have anything we can put into a truly wonderful funny book (similar to this one). The next lesson will take care of that.

Lesson #3

Combining funny ideas with funny drawings to make funny pictures.

Remember how in Lesson #1 we learned to think funny? And remember how in Lesson #2 we learned to draw funny? Well, we're now ready to put all these funny things together for one big hilarious and diverting funny thing like so . . .

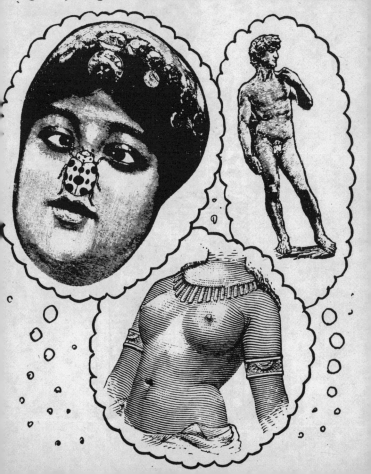

So remember, if you want to have the tremendous success that we just illustrated, always follow lessons #1, 2, and 3—in that order. Never switch around. For example, this is the unfunny disaster that could happen if you did. Supposing you switched around and did a funny picture first, like this . . .

And then you tried to get a funny idea. Then when you went to combine them, they'd come out like this and make absolutely no sense at all.

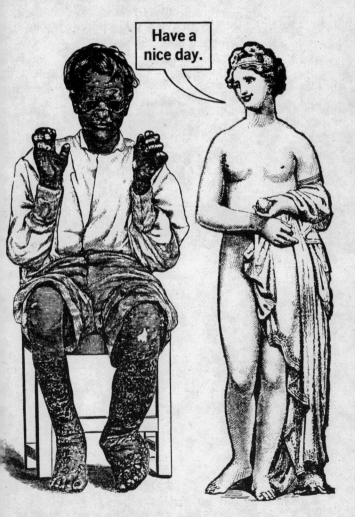

So be careful. Do this the way we taught you if you want to come up with truly funny stuff.

A SPACESHIP SAGA
THAT DOES NOT
GET OFF THE GROUND

④

Cartoon Folio Number One

23

THIS
SPACE
FOR
RENT

ASK FOR
OUR LOW
DAILY
RATES

A HOLDUP STORY
THAT'LL LET YOU DOWN

4

MORE

34

A BIT OF WISHFUL THINKING
YOU'LL WISH
YOU NEVER HEARD OF

(4)

Cartoon Folio Number Three

HOTEL

48

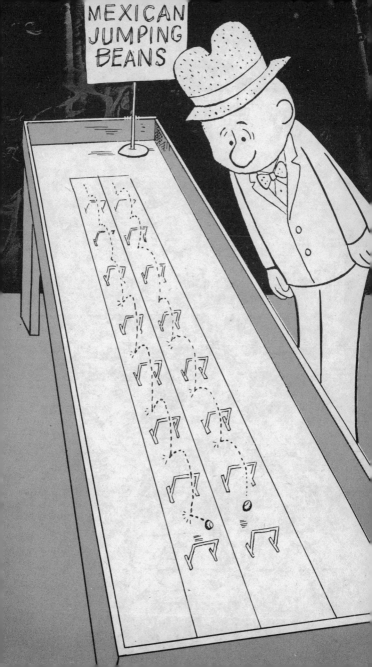

A FLOWER STORY
THAT WILTS BEFORE YOUR EYES

②

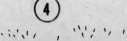

Cartoon Folio Number Four

SILENCE

60

A PIANO SAGA
THAT'S DEFINITELY OFF-KEY

MORE

Cartoon Folio Number Five

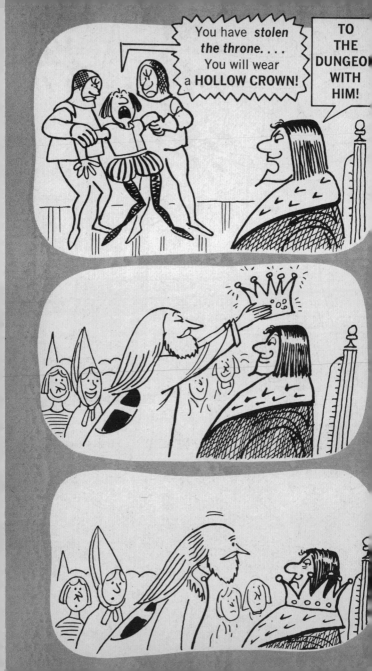

ATERNITY
NURSERY

A MARCHING PARADE
THAT SHOULD NOT BE REVIEWED

④

⑥

Cartoon Folio Number Six

A SHOOTOUT PLOT
THAT SIMPLY MISFIRED

②

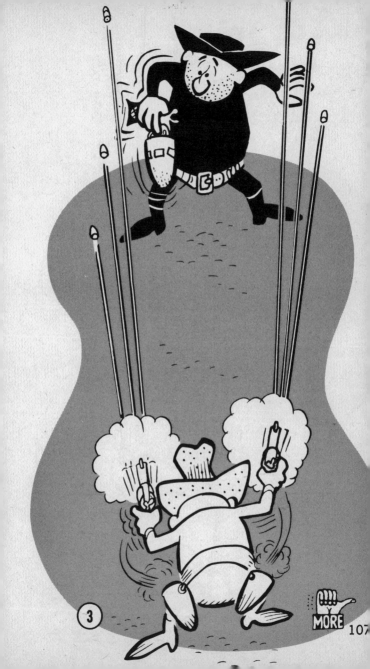

(4)

6

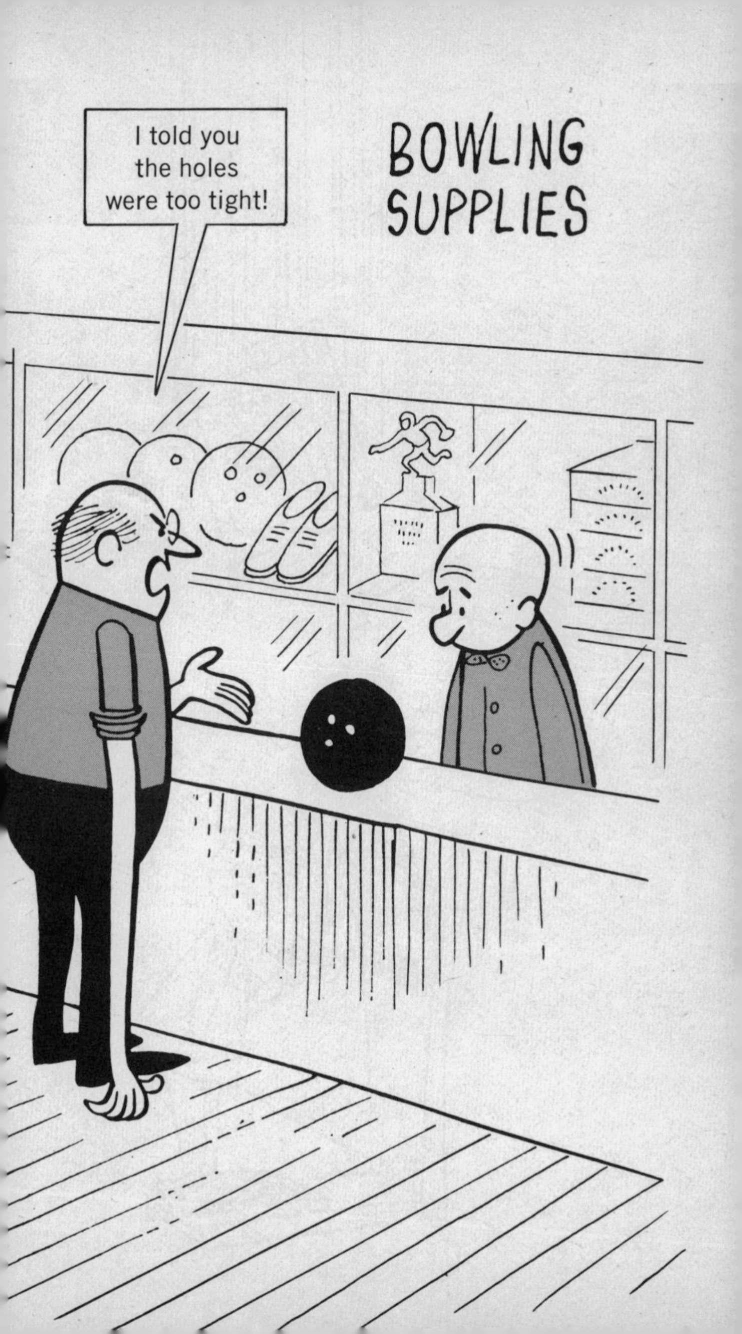
I told you the holes were too tight!
BOWLING SUPPLIES

A LANDLORD TALE
THAT SHOULD'VE BEEN EVICTED
FROM THIS BOOK

13 A

① MORE 117

②

125

Oh, I'd love to have your representative come over and explain your marvelous offer.

130

A GRAFFITI STORY
THAT'S RIGHT OFF THE WALL

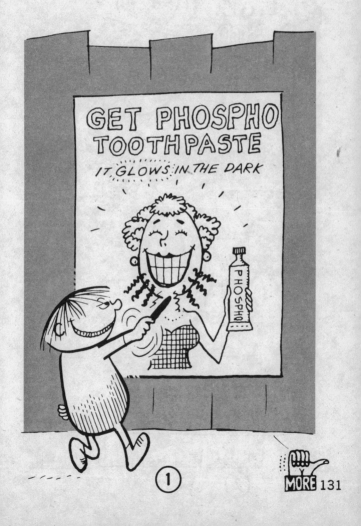

MORE

(2)

148

Cartoon Folio Number Eleven

A WRESTLING MATCH THAT'LL THROW YOU FOR A LOOP

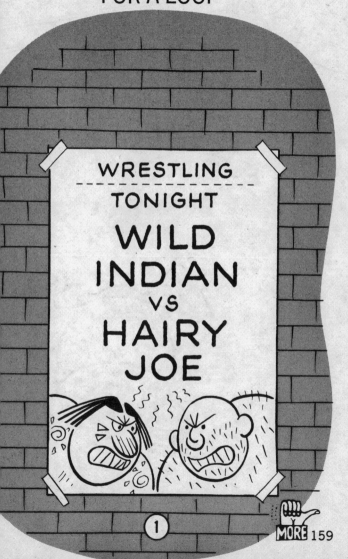

②

MORE

③

④

MORE 163

169

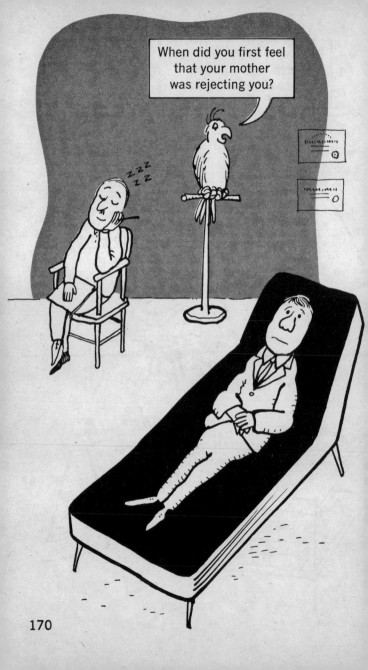

A HANDY STORY
TO TURN THUMBS DOWN ON

②

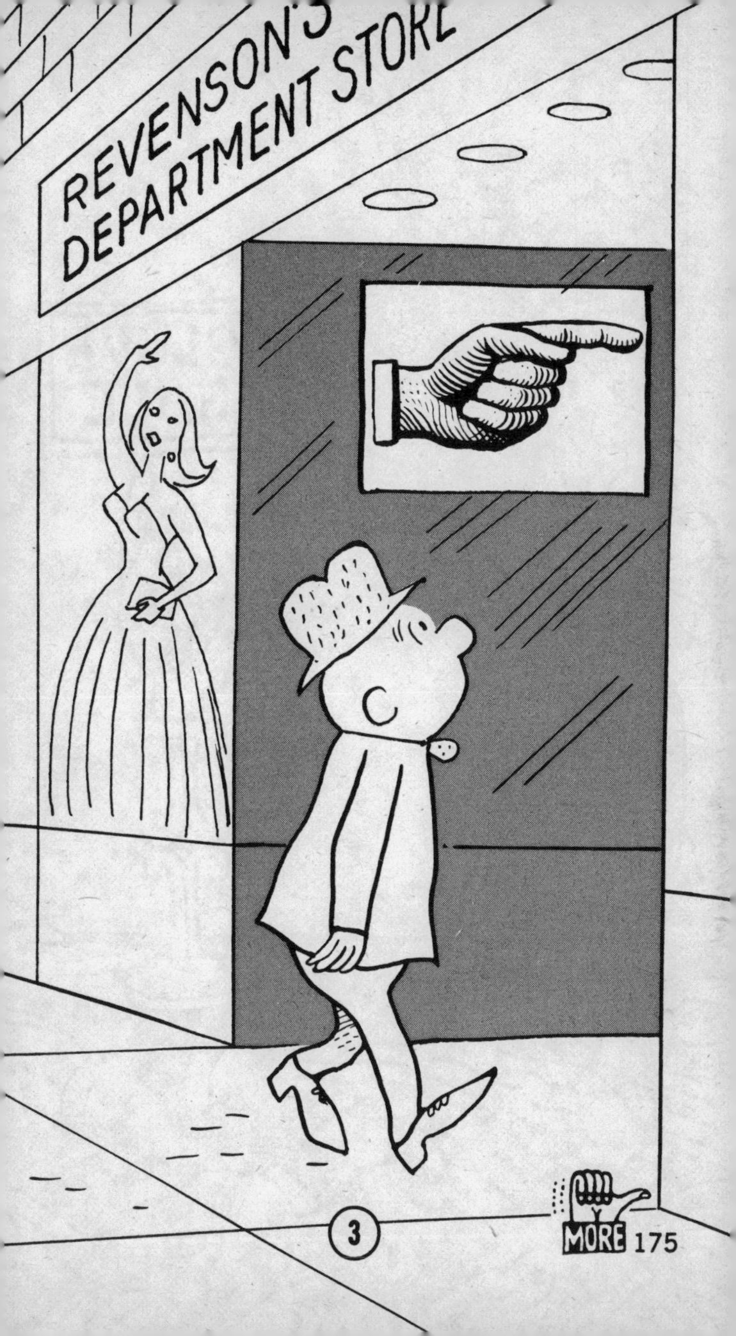
REVENSON'S
DEPARTMENT STORE
3
MORE

SHOP AT
NICK'S
PET
SHOP
----
40 MAIN ST.

A PUPPET SHOW
THAT COULD USE
A HELPING HAND

MORE 187

MORE

(6)